FAMOUS PEOPLE
FAMOUS LIVES

Biographies of famous people to
support the curriculum.

Saint
Patrick

by Nicola Baxter
Illustrations by Richard Morgan

W
FRANKLIN WATTS
NEW YORK • LONDON • SYDNEY

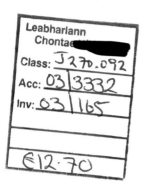
First published in 1999 by
Franklin Watts
96 Leonard Street
London
EC2A 4XD

Franklin Watts Australia
14 Mars Road
Lane Cove
NSW 2066

ISBN: 0 7496 3346 8

Dewey Decimal Classification Number: 270.092

A CIP catalogue record for this book
is available from the British Library.

Series editor: Sarah Ridley

Printed in Great Britain

Saint Patrick

Nearly two thousand years ago, the Romans conquered large parts of Britain. They ruled there for hundreds of years.

British people soon began to follow Roman customs. Some even learnt the Roman language, Latin.

In Roman Britain, people followed many religions. The Romans themselves prayed to lots of different gods. Some of them became Christians.

In about the year 389, somewhere in the west of Britain, a baby boy was born. He was given a Roman name, but today we know him as Patrick.

Patrick's family was Christian. In fact, his grandfather was a priest. Patrick was brought up in a comfortable house and had an easy life, but his teachers were not always happy with him!

The Romans ruled a huge empire. They did not have enough soldiers to keep watch over all their borders and were often under attack.

One day, Patrick's life suddenly changed.

Raiders from across the sea in Ireland landed near his home. They captured Patrick and carried him away.

In Ireland, Patrick was sold
to a chieftain called Milchu.
Everything was strange
and frightening.

No one spoke Latin. Here it was
not the Romans but the druids
who were powerful.

Now, Patrick really did have to work hard. Day after day, he was alone in the countryside, looking after the chieftain's cattle.

With no one to turn to but God, Patrick learnt how important it was to pray.

For six years, Patrick was a slave, but he never gave up hope. At night he dreamed that God was telling him he would one day be free.

At last, Patrick saw his chance
and ran away.

The runaway was in luck.

Patrick thanked God for giving him his freedom. When he reached France, he still had a long and difficult journey back to his home in Britain.

Patrick was happy to be home. But his time in Ireland had helped him decide to become a priest. He knew he had a lot to learn.

After a while, Patrick returned to France to find a monastery where he could study.

Learning was not easy for him, but he was determined to carry on. He felt that God had important work for him to do.

Patrick stayed in France for many years. He succeeded in becoming a priest. After many more years, he was made a bishop – an important figure in the Church.

But once again, Patrick dreamed that God had plans for him. He felt sure that he must return to Ireland.

There is work for you to do in Ireland.

In 432, Patrick's dream came true. The Pope sent him to Ireland as a missionary, to bring Christianity to the people there.

Patrick remembered a lot about
the beliefs of Irish people. He
knew that their religion was very
old. Nature and the seasons of
the year were important to them.

Patrick tried to show that
Christianity offered a new hope.

The druids were the leaders of the old Irish religion. They were against the Christian message.

Who does this Patrick think he is?

Every day Patrick was afraid he might be made a slave again, or even killed.

But Patrick's message began to be heard. He even converted his old master, Milchu.

Patrick travelled to Tara, in County Meath, where King Laoghaire had his court. He knew that the most powerful druids in the country would also be gathered there.

To celebrate Easter, Patrick lit an enormous bonfire on a hilltop. It was a huge challenge to the druids, for they were holding a ceremony of their own a few days later.

The custom was that no one lit
their bonfire before the king. But
Patrick was fearless in doing
what he felt was right.

After this, it is said that the
druids challenged Patrick
to a contest to see whether
Christian writings or druid
ones would survive.

When they pulled out the books, the druid writing had been washed away. The Christian message was still fresh and clear.

King Laoghaire's two daughters became Christians. When news of this spread, many others came to hear Patrick's message.

But it was not until he set up his headquarters at Armagh that Patrick began to feel the Church had a strong base in Ireland.

Many people found Christian ideas hard to understand. Patrick always tried to think of simple ways to explain them.

It is said that he used a shamrock leaf to show how God the Father, the Son and the Holy Spirit were different but the same.

Over the years, many legends have grown up about Saint Patrick and his life.

One tells how he ordered all the snakes in Ireland to leave.

Whether this really happened or not, it is true that today there are no snakes in Ireland!

Although Patrick had not found his own school days easy, he encouraged children to learn.

Patrick supported those who were called by God to be monks and nuns. He remembered when he too had first longed to offer his life to God.

We must all serve God in our own ways.

But he also believed that people could serve God in their everyday lives.

The writings that Patrick left behind him show that he was not a very learned man. But every word reveals his great love of God.

One of Patrick's most famous works is a hymn called *Saint Patrick's Breastplate*. It is full of simple faith and trust.

Saint Patrick's Breastplate

Christ be with me,
Christ within me,
Christ behind me,
Christ before me,
Christ beside me,
Christ to win me,
Christ to comfort and restore me.
Christ beneath me,
Christ above me,
Christ in quiet,
Christ in danger,
Christ in hearts of all that love me,
Christ in mouth of friend and stranger.

Prayer was always important to Patrick. When he was an old man, he went to County Mayo for forty days of quiet prayer and closeness with God.

Patrick died at Saul in County Down in 461. He was over seventy. Today he still has a very special place in the hearts of Irish people.

Further facts

Latin

Although the Roman Empire collapsed during Patrick's lifetime, the Latin language continued to be important in Europe for centuries. It was the language of learning.

Today, doctors still use Latin terms to describe parts of the body. Scientists use Latin names for all living things, so that they can be clear when talking to other scientists in different parts of the world.

Saint Patrick in New York

In the 1800s, there was a terrible famine in Ireland. Thousands of people fled to the United States of America. They landed in New York, and many of them stayed there.

That is why today the Roman Catholic cathedral in New York is called Saint Patrick's, and on March 17 each year, there is an enormous Saint Patrick's Day parade.

Some important dates in Saint Patrick's lifetime

About 389 Patrick is born in the west of Britain.

403 Patrick is captured by raiders and taken to Ireland as a slave.

409 Patrick escapes on a ship to France. He returns briefly to Britain but then returns to France to study in the monastery of Lérins. Later he studies at Auxerre under Saint Germanus, who makes him a bishop.

432 Patrick returns to Ireland as a missionary. For years he fears for his life as he works to spread Christianity.

454 The real beginning of the Christian Church in Ireland, as Patrick makes Armagh his base.

461 Patrick dies in Ireland, at Saul, County Down.